A NIGHT

A Play

by

HAROLD PINTER

SAMUEL  FRENCH

LONDON

NEW YORK   TORONTO   SYDNEY   HOLLYWOOD

A NIGHT OUT

Produced by Caravel Productions Ltd, by arrangement with New Watergate Presentations Ltd at the Comedy Theatre, London, on the 2nd October 1961, with the following cast of characters:

(in the order of their appearance)

ALBERT STOKES, an insurance clerk	*Brian Peck*
MRS STOKES, his mother	*Anna Wing*
SEELEY, a clerk	*Rodney Bewes*
KEDGE, a clerk	*Walter Hall*
BARMAN	*Douglas Harris*
OLD MAN	*Peter Hutton*
MR KING	*Trevor Reid*
MR RYAN	*William Stephens*
GIDNEY	*Glyn Houston*
JOYCE	*Patricia Marks*
EILEEN	*Patricia Denys*
BETTY	*Gabrielle Beaumont*
HORNE	*Nicholas Pennell*
BARROW	*Michael Slater*
"THE GIRL"	*Jeanne Mockford*

Directed by LEILA BLAKE

Setting designed by BRIAN CURRAH

SYNOPSIS OF SCENES

The action is continuous and takes place during one evening in London

SCENE I	The kitchen of Mrs Stokes' house
SCENE II	A coffee-stall
SCENE III	The kitchen
SCENE IV	The coffee-stall
SCENE V	The lounge of Mr King's house
SCENE VI	The kitchen
SCENE VII	The coffee-stall
SCENE VIII	The "Girl's" room
SCENE IX	The kitchen

Time—the present

A NIGHT OUT

A composite setting with the coffee-stall R, *the "Girl's" room on a rostrum back* C *and the kitchen* L. *The kitchen is furnished with a sink and draining-board at the back, a gas stove and kitchen cabinet* L, *and a small table* C, *with upright chairs above and* L *of it. Between the sink and the stove there are two or three steps leading up and off* L *to a small landing, and thence to the hall and bedrooms. The "Girl's" bedroom up* C *is entered by an arch at the back and is furnished with a divan bed up* R *with an upright chair below it, a small piece of carpet, a gas-fire up* L, *with a mantelpiece over it and a stool with an embroidered top* L. *The coffee-stall* R *is mounted on one half of a circular revolving truck, the back half carrying a semicircular bar for use in the lounge party scene. A wooden bench for use by the coffee-stall customers is* C. *For the lounge party scene, the truck is revolved to display the bar, the wooden bench is reset* RC, *up and down stage, an armchair is set* LC, *and a sofa is set down* L. *Three high stools are set in front of the bar.*

SCENE I

SCENE—*The kitchen of Mrs Stokes' small house in the South of London.*

When the CURTAIN *rises, the lights come up on the kitchen. It is a small room, clean and tidy. The table is set for two.* ALBERT STOKES, *an insurance clerk, aged twenty-eight, is standing in his shirt and trousers, combing his hair in a mirror on the shelf over the draining-board. The whistle and sounds of a train passing are heard.*

MRS STOKES (*off; calling*) Albert!

(ALBERT *ignores the call and brushes his hair*)

(*Off; calling*) Albert!

(ALBERT *slips the comb in his pocket, bends down, reaches under the draining-board, takes out a shoe-duster, puts his foot up on the chair* L *of the table and polishes his shoes.*

MRS STOKES *enters from the landing and crosses to* R *of the table*)

Albert, I've been calling you. (*She watches him*) What are you doing?

ALBERT. Nothing.

MRS STOKES. Didn't you hear me call you, Albert? I've been calling you from upstairs.

ALBERT. You seen my tie?

MRS STOKES. Oh, I say, I'll have to put the flag out.

ALBERT. What do you mean?

MRS STOKES. Cleaning your shoes, Albert? I'll have to put the flag out, won't I?

(ALBERT *puts the duster on the table and turns and looks on the kitchen cabinet*)

(*She picks up the duster, replaces it under the draining-board then turns to Albert*) What are you looking for?

ALBERT. My tie. The striped one, the blue one.

MRS STOKES. The bulb's gone in grandma's room.

ALBERT. Has it?

MRS STOKES. That's what I was calling you about. I went in and switched on the light and the bulb had gone. Aren't those your best trousers, Albert? What have you put on your best trousers for?

ALBERT (*crossing to Mrs Stokes*) Look, Mum, where's my tie? The blue one, the blue tie, where is it? You know the one I mean, the blue striped one, I gave it to you this morning.

MRS STOKES. What do you want your tie for?

ALBERT. I want to put it on. I asked you to press it for me this morning. I gave it to you this morning before I went to work, didn't I?

MRS STOKES (*moving to the gas stove; gently*) Well, your dinner'll be ready soon. You can look for it afterwards. (*She opens the oven door for a moment and peers in*) Lay the table, there's a good boy.

ALBERT. Why should I look for it afterwards? You know where it is now.

MRS STOKES. You've got five minutes. Go down to the cellar, Albert, get a bulb and put it in grandma's room. Go on.

ALBERT (*moving below the table; irritably*) I don't know why you keep calling that room grandma's room, she's been dead ten years.

MRS STOKES (*moving to the kitchen cabinet*) Albert!

ALBERT. I mean, it's just a junk room, that's all it is.

MRS STOKES. Albert, that's no way to speak about your grandma, you know that as well as I do.

ALBERT. I'm not saying a word against grandma . . .

MRS STOKES. You'll upset me in a minute, you go on like that.

ALBERT. I'm not going on about anything.

MRS STOKES. Yes, you are. Now, why don't you go and put a bulb in grandma's room and by the time you come down I'll have your dinner on the table.

ALBERT. I can't go down to the cellar, I've got my best trousers on. I've got a white shirt on.

MRS STOKES (*crossing to Albert*) You're dressing up tonight, aren't you? Dressing up, cleaning your shoes, anyone would think you were going to the *Ritz.*

ALBERT. I'm not going to the *Ritz.*

MRS STOKES (*suspiciously*) What do you mean—you're not going to the *Ritz?*

ALBERT. What do you mean?

MRS STOKES. The way you said you're not going to the *Ritz,* it sounded like you were going somewhere else.

ALBERT (*wearily*) I am.

MRS STOKES (*with shocked surprise*) You're going out?

ALBERT (*moving to the draining-board*) You know I'm going out.

(MRS STOKES *follows Albert*)

I told you I was going out. I told you last week. I told you this morning. Look, where's my tie? I've got to have my tie. I'm late already. Come on, Mum, where'd you put it?

MRS STOKES. What about your dinner?

ALBERT (*moving and searching on the kitchen cabinet*) Look—I told you—I haven't got the . . . (*He finds the tie*) Wait a minute—ah, here it is.

MRS STOKES. You can't wear that tie. I haven't pressed it.

ALBERT. You have. Look at it. Of course you have. It's beautifully pressed. It's fine. (*He puts his tie on and knots it*)

MRS STOKES (*moving to Albert*) Where are you going?

ALBERT. Mum, I've told you, honestly, three times. Honestly, I've told you three times I had to go out tonight.

MRS STOKES. No, you didn't.

(ALBERT *exclaims and knots his tie*)

I thought you were joking.

ALBERT (*turning and facing her*) I'm not going . . . I'm just going to Mr King's. I've told you. You just don't believe me.

MRS STOKES. You're going to Mr King's?

ALBERT. Mr Ryan's leaving. You know Ryan. He's leaving the firm. He's been there years. So Mr King's giving a sort of party for him at his house—well, not exactly a party, not a party, just a few—you know—anyway, we're all invited. I've got to go. Everyone else is going. I've got to go. I don't want to go, but I've got to.

MRS STOKES (*sitting above the table; bewildered*) Well, I don't know . . .

ALBERT (*putting an arm around her*) I won't be late. I don't want to go. I'd much rather stay with you.

MRS STOKES. Would you?

ALBERT. You know I would. Who wants to go to Mr King's party?

MRS STOKES. We were going to have our game of cards.

ALBERT. Well, we can't have our game of cards.

(*There is a pause*)

MRS STOKES. Put the bulb in grandma's room, Albert.

ALBERT (*moving to the draining-board*) I've told you I'm not going down to the cellar in my white shirt. (*He moves to

R *of the table*) There's no light in the cellar, either. I'll be pitch black in five minutes, looking for those bulbs.

MRS STOKES. I told you to put a light in the cellar. I told you yesterday.

ALBERT (*moving behind her*) Well, I can't do it now.

MRS STOKES. If we had a light in the cellar you'd be able to see where those bulbs were. (*She rises*) You don't expect me to go down to the cellar?

ALBERT. I don't know why we keep bulbs in the cellar!

(*There is a pause*)

MRS STOKES (*turning away*) Your father would turn in his grave if he heard you raise your voice to me. You're all I've got, Albert. I want you to remember that. I haven't got anyone else. I want you—I want you to bear that in mind.

ALBERT (*with a step towards her*) I'm sorry—I raised my voice. (*He moves on to the landing. Mumbling*) I've got to go.

MRS STOKES (*following Albert*) Albert.

ALBERT. What?

MRS STOKES. I want to ask you a question.

ALBERT. What?

MRS STOKES. Are you leading a clean life?

ALBERT. A clean life?

MRS STOKES. You're not leading an unclean life, are you?

ALBERT. What are you talking about?

MRS STOKES. You're not messing about with girls, are you? You're not going to be messing about with girls tonight?

ALBERT (*moving to L of the table*) Don't be so ridiculous!

MRS STOKES. Answer me, Albert. I'm your mother.

ALBERT. I don't know any girls.

MRS STOKES. If you're going to the firm's party, there'll be girls there, won't there? Girls from the office?

ALBERT. I don't like them, any of them.

MRS STOKES. You promise?

ALBERT. Promise what?

MRS STOKES. That—that you won't upset your father.

ALBERT (*turning to her*) My father? How can I upset my

father? You're always talking about upsetting people who
are dead.

MRS STOKES. Oh, Albert, you don't know how you hurt
me, you don't know the hurtful way you've got, speaking of
your poor father like that.

ALBERT. But he is dead.

MRS STOKES. He's not. He's living. (*She touches her breast*)
In here. And this is his house.

(*There is a pause*)

ALBERT. Look, Mum, I won't be late—and I won't . . .

MRS STOKES. But what about your dinner? (*She goes to
the gas stove*) It's nearly ready.

ALBERT. Seeley and Kedge are waiting for me. I told
you not to cook dinner this morning. (*He moves to the stairs*)
Just because you never listen . . .

(ALBERT *exits up the stairs*)

MRS STOKES (*crossing to the stairs and calling*) Well, what
am I going to do while you're out? I can't go into grandma's room because there's no light. I can't go down to
the cellar in the dark—we were going to have a game of
cards—it's Friday night—what about our game of rummy?

The LIGHTS *fade on the kitchen and come up on the coffee-
stall* R.

SCENE II

SCENE—*A coffee-stall by a railway arch.*

When the LIGHTS *come up,* SEELEY *is standing at the counter.*
KEDGE *is sitting on the bench. An* OLD MAN *leans on the
upstage corner of the counter. The* BARMAN *is serving Seeley
with two cups of tea.*

SEELEY. Give us a cheese roll as well, will you?

KEDGE. Make it two.

SEELEY. Make it two.

BARMAN (*lifting the glass cover*) Two cheese rolls.

SEELEY. What are these—sausages?

BARMAN. Best *pork* sausages.

SEELEY (*to Kedge*) You want a sausage?

KEDGE (*shuddering*) No, thanks.

SEELEY (*looking at the sausages*) Yes, you're right.

BARMAN (*putting two cheese rolls on a plate*) Two cheese rolls. What about these sausages, you want them or don't you?

SEELEY. Just the rolls, mate.

BARMAN. Two teas, two rolls, makes one and eightpence.

(SEELEY *gives the Barman half a crown, then hands a cup of tea and a roll to Kedge*)

KEDGE. There'll be plenty to eat at the party. (*He starts to eat*)

SEELEY. I'll bet. (*He sips his tea*)

OLD MAN. Eh!

(*The others look at the Old Man*)

(*To Seeley*) Your mate was by here not long ago.

SEELEY. Which mate?

OLD MAN. He had a cup of tea, didn't he, Fred? Sitting over there, he was, on the bench. He said he was going home to change, but to tell you he'd be back.

KEDGE. Uh-uh!

OLD MAN. Not gone more than above forty-five minutes.

BARMAN (*giving Seeley his change*) One and eight from half a dollar leaves you ten pennies.

OLD MAN. Anyway, he told me to tell you when I see you he was coming back.

KEDGE. Thanks very much.

SEELEY (*crossing to Kedge*) Well, I hope he won't be long. I don't want to miss the booze.

KEDGE. You think there'll be much there, do you?

OLD MAN. Yes, he was sitting over there.

KEDGE (*rising and crossing to the counter*) Who was?

OLD MAN. Your mate.

SEELEY. Oh, yes.

OLD MAN. Yes, sitting over there, he was. Took his cup of tea and went and sat down, didn't he, Fred? He sat there looking very compressed with himself.

KEDGE. Very what?

OLD MAN. Compressed. I thought he was looking compressed, didn't you, Fred?

BARMAN. Depressed. He means depressed.

SEELEY (*crossing to the bench*) No wonder. What about that game on Saturday, eh?

KEDGE. You were going to tell me. You haven't told me yet.

BARMAN. What game? Fulham?

SEELEY. No, the firm. Firm's got a team, see? Play on Saturdays.

BARMAN. Who'd you play?

SEELEY (*crossing to the counter*) Other firms.

BARMAN. You boys in the team, are you?

KEDGE. Yes. I've been off sick, though. I didn't play last week.

BARMAN. Sick, eh? You want to try one of my sausages, don't he, Henry?

OLD MAN. Oh, ay, yes.

> (KEDGE *sitting*.
> SEELEY *crosses to the bench and sits beside Kedge*)

KEDGE. What happened with the game, then?

SEELEY. Well, when you couldn't play, Gidney moved Albert to left back.

KEDGE. He's a left half.

SEELEY. I know he's a left half. I said to Gidney myself I said to him, "Look, why don't you go to left back, Gidney?" He said, "No, I'm too valuable at centre half."

KEDGE. He didn't, did he?

SEELEY. Yes. Well, you know who was on the right wing, don't you? Connor.

KEDGE. Who? Tony Connor?

SEELEY. No. You know Connor. What's the matter with you? You've played against Connor yourself.

KEDGE. Oh—what's-his-name—Micky Connor.

SEELEY. Yes.

KEDGE. I thought he'd given up the game.

SEELEY. No, what are you talking about. He plays for the printing works, plays outside right for the printing works.

KEDGE. He's a good ball-player, that Connor, isn't he?

SEELEY. Look. I said to Albert before the kick-off, "Connor's on the right wing," I said, "play your normal game." I told him six times before the kick-off.

KEDGE. What's the good of him playing his normal game? He's a left half, he's not a left back.

SEELEY. Yes, but he's a defensive left half, isn't he? That's why I told him to play his normal game. "You don't want to worry about Connor," I said, "he's a good ball-player but he's not all that good."

KEDGE. Oh, he's good, though.

SEELEY (*rising and crossing to* R) No-one's denying he's good. But he's not all that good. I mean, he's not tip-top. You know what I mean?

KEDGE. He's fast.

SEELEY. He's fast, but he's not all that fast, is he?

KEDGE (*doubtfully*) Well, not all that fast . . .

SEELEY. What about Levy? Was Levy fast?

KEDGE. Well, Levy was a sprinter.

SEELEY. He was a dasher, Levy. All he knew was run.

KEDGE. He could move.

SEELEY. Yes, but look how Albert played him. He cut him off, he played him out the game. And Levy's faster than Connor.

KEDGE. Yes, but he wasn't so clever, though.

SEELEY (*crossing to the bench*) Well, what about Foxall?

KEDGE. Who? Lou Foxall?

SEELEY (*putting his foot up on the bench*) No, you're talking about Lou Fox, I'm talking about Sandy Foxall.

KEDGE. Oh, the winger.

SEELEY. Sure. He was a very smart ball-player—Foxall. But what did Albert do? He played his normal game. He let him come. He waited for him. And Connor's not as clever as Foxall.

KEDGE. He's clever, though.

SEELEY (*taking his foot off the bench*) Gawd blimey, I know he's clever, but he's not as clever as Foxall, is he?

KEDGE. The trouble is, with Connor, he's fast, too, isn't he?

SEELEY. But if Albert would have played his normal game . . . He played a game foreign to him.

KEDGE. How many'd Connor get?

SEELEY. Connor? (*He sits on the bench*) He made three and scored two.

(*There is a pause. They eat*)

KEDGE. No wonder he's depressed, old Albert.

SEELEY. Oh, he was very depressed after the game, I can tell you. And of course Gidney was after him, of course. You know Gidney.

KEDGE. That birk.

(*There is a pause*)

OLD MAN. Yes, he was sitting over where you are now, wasn't he, Fred? Looking very compressed with himself, very, very compressed, I thought.

The LIGHTS fade on the coffee-stall and come up on the kitchen

SCENE III

SCENE—*The kitchen.*

When the LIGHTS come up, MRS STOKES is tidying up at the dresser. ALBERT enters on the landing. He is wearing his jacket.

MRS STOKES (*calling*) Albert! Where are you going?

ALBERT (*stopping and turning*) Out.

MRS STOKES (*moving to the gas stove*) Your dinner's ready.

ALBERT. I'm sorry. I haven't got time to have it.

MRS STOKES. Look at your suit. (*She moves to Albert*) You're not going out with your suit in that state, are you?

ALBERT. What's the matter with it? (*He moves to R of the table*)

MRS STOKES. It needs a good brush, that's what's the matter with it. You can't go out like that. Come on, come here and I'll give it a brush.

ALBERT. It's all right . . .

MRS STOKES (*taking a clothes brush from the cabinet*) Come on.

(ALBERT *moves to Mrs Stokes*)

(*She brushes*) Turn round. No, stand still. You can't go out and disgrace me, Albert. If you've got to go out you've got to look nice. There, that's better. (*She replaces the brush on the cabinet, then straightens Albert's tie*) I didn't tell you what I made for you, did I? I made it specially. I made shepherd's pie tonight.

ALBERT (*taking her hand from his tie*) The tie's all right. (*He goes on to the landing*) Well, ta-ta.

MRS STOKES (*moving to him*) Albert! Wait a minute. Where's your handkerchief?

ALBERT. What handkerchief?

MRS STOKES. You haven't got a handkerchief in your breast pocket.

ALBERT. That doesn't matter, does it?

MRS STOKES. Doesn't matter? I should say it does matter. Just a minute. (*She takes a handkerchief from the cabinet*) Here you are. A nice clean one. (*She arranges it in his pocket*) You mustn't let me down, you know. You've got to be properly dressed. Your father was always properly dressed. You'd never see him out without a handkerchief in his breast pocket. He always looked like a gentleman.

ALBERT *exits as—*

the LIGHTS *fade on the kitchen and come up on the coffee-stall*

SCENE IV

SCENE—*The coffee-stall.*

When the LIGHTS *come up,* SEELEY *is sitting on the bench. The* BARMAN *is behind the counter. The* OLD MAN *is leaning at the upstage corner of the counter.* KEDGE *is returning the tea-cups to the counter.*

KEDGE. Time we were there.

SEELEY. We'll give him five minutes.

KEDGE. I bet his mum's combing his hair for him, eh? (*He crosses to the bench and sits*) You ever met her, Seeley?

SEELEY. Who?

KEDGE. His—mother.

SEELEY. Yes.

KEDGE. What's she like?

SEELEY (*shortly*) She's all right.

KEDGE. All right, is she? (*He takes out a packet of cigarettes and a lighter*)

SEELEY. I told you. I just said she was all right.

(*There is a pause as* KEDGE *lights a cigarette for himself*)

KEDGE. No, what I mean is, he always gets a bit niggly when she's mentioned, doesn't he? A bit touchy. You noticed that?

SEELEY (*unwillingly*) Yes.

KEDGE. Why's that, then?

SEELEY. I don't know. What're you asking for?

KEDGE. I don't know. I just thought you might—sort of—well, I mean, you know him better than I do, don't you? (*He pauses*) Of course, he don't let much slip, does he, old Albert?

SEELEY. No, not much.

KEDGE. He's a bit deep really, isn't he?

SEELEY. Yes, he's a bit deep.

KEDGE (*after a pause*) Secretive.

SEELEY (*irritably*) What do you mean—secretive? What are you talking about?

KEDGE. I was just saying he was secretive.

SEELEY (*rising*) What are you talking about? What do you mean—he's secretive?

KEDGE. You said yourself he was deep.

SEELEY. I said he was deep. I didn't say he was secretive.

(ALBERT *enters down* L *and crosses to the coffee-stall*)

KEDGE (*rising*) Hullo, Albert.

ALBERT. Hullo.

KEDGE (*moving backwards down* R) That's a nice bit of clobber you've got on there.

SEELEY. Very fair, very fair.

KEDGE. Yes, fits you like a glove.

SEELEY (*taking Albert's arm*) Well, come on, catch a thirty-six round the corner.

ALBERT. Wait a minute, I—I don't think I feel like going, actually.

KEDGE (*crossing to Albert*) What are you talking about?

ALBERT. I don't feel like it, that's all.

SEELEY. What, with all that drink laid on?

ALBERT (*sitting on the bench*) No, I've just got a bit of a headache.

OLD MAN. That's the bloke. That's the bloke was here before, isn't it, Fred? (*To Albert*) I gave them your message, son.

ALBERT. Oh—thanks.

OLD MAN (*to the others*) Didn't I?

KEDGE (*moving above the bench*) You did, you did, mate.

SEELEY. Well, what's going on, you coming or what?

ALBERT. No, I feel a bit—you know . . .

KEDGE (*moving in close behind Albert*) Don't you know who'll be there tonight, Albert?

ALBERT. Who?

KEDGE. Joyce.

ALBERT. Joyce? Well, what about it?

KEDGE. And Eileen.

ALBERT. Well, so what?

KEDGE. And Betty. Betty'll be there. They'll all be there.

SEELEY. Betty? Who's Betty?

KEDGE. Betty? What do you mean? You don't know Betty?

SEELEY. There's no girl in the office called Betty.

KEDGE. Betty. The dark bit. The new one. The one that come in last week. The little one, in the corner.

SEELEY. Oh, her. Is her name Betty? I thought it was . . .

KEDGE. Betty. Her name's Betty.

SEELEY. I've been calling her Hetty.

(*There is a pause*)

KEDGE. Anyway, she'll be there. (*He moves between Seeley and Albert*) She's raring to go, that one.

ALBERT. Well, you go, then, I'll . . .

KEDGE. Albert, what's the matter with you, mate? It's wine, women and song tonight.

ALBERT. I see them every day, don't I? What's new in that?

KEDGE. You frightened Gidney'll be after you, then, because of the game?

ALBERT. What do you mean?

KEDGE. Go on, everyone has a bad game, Albert.

ALBERT. Yes, they do, don't they?

KEDGE. I played against Connor myself once. He's tricky. He's a very tricky ball-player.

ALBERT. Yes.

SEELEY. Clever player, Connor.

ALBERT (*rising*) What's Gidney got to do with it, Kedge?

KEDGE. Well, you know what he is.

ALBERT. What?

KEDGE. Well, he's captain of the team, isn't he, for a bang-off?

ALBERT. You think . . . ?

SEELEY. Oh, scrub round it, will you? It's late.

ALBERT. You think I'm frightened of Gidney?

KEDGE. I didn't say you were.

SEELEY. Gidney's all right. What's the matter with Gidney?

ALBERT. Yes. What's wrong with him?

KEDGE. Nothing. There's nothing wrong with him. He's a nice bloke. He's a charmer, isn't he?

SEELEY. The cream of the cream. Well, come on, you coming or what?

ALBERT. Yes, all right. I'll come.

SEELEY. Just a minute. (*He moves to the counter*) I'll get some fags.

(KEDGE *and* ALBERT *turn away*)

(*To the Barman*) Twenty Weights, mate.

(*The* BARMAN *looks on his shelf*)

KEDGE (*regarding Albert*) How's your mum, Albert?
ALBERT. All right.
KEDGE. That's the idea.
BARMAN (*turning*) Only got Woods.
SEELEY. They'll do.
ALBERT (*quietly*) What do you mean, how's my mum?

(*The* BARMAN *hands Seeley a packet of cigarettes.* SEELEY *pays*)

KEDGE. I just asked how she was, that's all.
ALBERT. Why shouldn't she be all right?
KEDGE. I didn't say she wasn't.
ALBERT. Well, she is.
KEDGE. Well, that's all right, then, isn't it?
ALBERT. What are you getting at?
KEDGE. I don't know what's the matter with you tonight, Albert.
SEELEY (*moving to Albert and Kedge*) What's up now?
ALBERT. Kedge here, suddenly asking how my mother is.
KEDGE. Just a friendly question, that's all. Caw! (*He turns away*) You can't even ask a bloke how his mother is now without him getting niggly.
ALBERT. Well, why's he suddenly ask . . . ?
SEELEY. He was just asking a friendly question, mate. What's the matter with you?
ALBERT (*after a pause*) Oh.
SEELEY. Well, how is she, then?
ALBERT. She's fine. What about yours?
SEELEY. Fine. Fine.
KEDGE (*after a pause*) Mine's fine, too, you know. Great. Absolutely great. A marvel for her age, my mother is. Of course, she had me very late.

(*There is a pause*)

SEELEY (*crossing below the others and turning*) Well? Are you coming or not? Or what?

KEDGE (*moving to Seeley*) I'm coming.
ALBERT (*following Kedge*) I'm coming.

SEELEY, KEDGE and ALBERT exit as—

the LIGHTS BLACK-OUT

SCENE V

SCENE—*The lounge of Mr King's house.*
    The truck R *is revolved revealing the bar and counter with drinks and glasses. The bench* C *is set* RC, *up and down stage. The armchair from the rostrum is set* LC *and a sofa is set* L. *Three tall stools are in front of the bar.*

When the LIGHTS *come up, the party is in progress. Music of a Quick Step is heard.* MR RYAN, *an old man, is seated on the bench* RC. JOYCE *and* EILEEN *are seated on stools at the bar.* KEDGE *and* BETTY *are dancing up* RC. SEELEY *and* ALBERT *are standing together near the sofa* L. BARROW *and* HORNE *are standing at the upstage end of the bar.*

JOYCE. You enjoying the party, Mr Ryan?

    (RYAN *nods and smiles*)

EILEEN (*pleasantly*) Enjoying the party, are you?

    (RYAN *nods, winks and smiles.*
        MR KING *and* GIDNEY *enter up* LC *and move to the sofa.* KING *is an urbane man in his fifties.* GIDNEY, *the chief accountant, is in his late twenties*)

KING (*to Gidney*) I recommend a bicycle, honestly. It really keeps you up to the mark. Out in the morning, on the bike, through the town—the air in your lungs, muscles working—you arrive at work—you arrive at work fresh—you know what I mean? Uplifted.
GIDNEY. Not so good in the rain.
KING. Refreshes you. Clears the cobwebs. (*He laughs*)

    (KEDGE *and* BETTY *dance down* C)

SEELEY. You don't walk to work, do you, Gidney?

GIDNEY. Me? I've got the car.

KING. I drive, too, of course, but I often think seriously of taking up cycling again. I often think very seriously about it, you know.

KEDGE (*to Betty; as they dance*) You dance like a dream, Betty, you know that?

BETTY (*shyly*) I don't.

KEDGE. You do. Honest. Like a dream. Like a dream come true.

BETTY. You're just saying that.

KING (*to Seeley*) Well, Kedge looks all right again, doesn't he? What was the matter with him? I've forgotten.

(KEDGE *and* BETTY *dance down* L)

KING. Not enough exercise. (*To Kedge*) You'll have to see you get more exercise, Kedge.

KEDGE. You never said a truer word, Mr King.

(KEDGE *and* BETTY *dance to* R)

SEELEY. Well, he don't look in bad trim to me, Mr King.

(KING *and* SEELEY *laugh*)

KING. I must admit it.

(KEDGE *and* BETTY *dance off down* R)

GIDNEY (*moving behind the sofa*) He'll never get to the last lap with that one, I can tell you.

(RYAN *rises and crosses to* King)

KING (*smiling*) Now, now, you young men, that's quite enough of that. No more of that. (*He turns to Ryan*) Ah, Mr Ryan—come and sit down and make yourself comfortable.

(KING *takes* RYAN *by the arm and sits him in the armchair* LC. *The dance music ceases*)

GIDNEY (*to Albert; pleasantly*) What are you laughing at, Stokes?

ALBERT. What?

GIDNEY. Sorry. I thought you were laughing.

ALBERT. I was laughing. You made a joke.

GIDNEY. Oh, yes, of course. Sorry. (*He pauses*) Well, we've got Kedge back at left back next Saturday.

SEELEY. That's a lovely pair of shoes you're wearing, Gidney.

GIDNEY. Do you think so?

(*Samba music is heard*)

SEELEY. Oh, they're the best, the very best, aren't they, Albert? Gidney always wears a nice pair of shoes, doesn't he, you noticed that? That's one thing I'll say about you, Gidney—you carry your feet well.

EILEEN (*rising and crossing to* C) A samba. Who's going to dance?

SEELEY (*crossing to Eileen*) I'll give it a trot.

(SEELEY *and* EILEEN *dance up* LC)

GIDNEY. Don't you dance, Stokes?

ALBERT. Yes, sometimes.

GIDNEY. Do you? You will excuse me, won't you? (*He crosses to Joyce*)

ALBERT. Yes. (*He is left standing alone*)

KING. Well, Ryan, enjoying the party?

(RYAN *nods and smiles*)

Nice to see a lot of young people enjoying themselves, eh?

(RYAN *nods and smiles*)

Of course, it's all in your honour, old man. Let's fill you up. I'll be the oldest man in the office after you've gone.

(RYAN *rises. He and* KING *move to the bar where* KING *pours a drink for Ryan.* JOYCE *rises and moves with* GIDNEY *below the bench* RC, *where they whisper together*)

JOYCE. No. Why should I?

GIDNEY. Go on. Just for a lark.

JOYCE. What for?

GIDNEY. For a lark. Just for a lark.

JOYCE. You've got an evil mind, you have.

GIDNEY. No, it'll amuse me, that's all. I feel like being amused.

JOYCE (*sitting on the downstage end of the bench* RC) Well, I'm not going to.

GIDNEY. Gah, you wouldn't know how to, anyway.

JOYCE. Oh, wouldn't I?

GIDNEY (*taking her arm*) Get hold of Eileen, don't tell her I told you, though, and go over and lead him a dance, just lead him a dance, that's all, see what he does. I want to see his reaction, that's all, I just want to see how he takes it.

JOYCE. What, in front of everyone else, in front of . . . ?

GIDNEY. Just talk to him, talk to him. I don't mean anything else, do I?

JOYCE. What do I get if I do?

GIDNEY. A toffee apple.

JOYCE. Oh, really? Thank you.

GIDNEY. I'll take you for a ride in the car. Honest.

(SEELEY *and* EILEEN *dance* C)

SEELEY (*as they dance*) Hullo, Mr Ryan. Enjoying the party?

EILEEN (*to Seeley*) You dance well, don't you?

SEELEY. I was going in for ballet once.

EILEEN. Go on!

SEELEY. Yes, true. They offered me the leading part in *Rigoletto*. When I was a boy soprano.

EILEEN. You're making it up.

(SEELEY *and* EILEEN *dance off* R)

GIDNEY (*to Joyce*) No, he just irritates me, that bloke. I —I haven't got any time for a bloke like that.

JOYCE. He's just quiet, that's all.

(KEDGE *and* BETTY *enter down* R *and move up* C. KING *moves to Betty.* RYAN *crosses and sits in the armchair* LC)

GIDNEY. Well, see if you can wake him up.

KING (*to Betty*) Well, Miss Todd, it hasn't taken you long to get to know everyone, has it?

BETTY. Oh, no, Mr King.

KEDGE. I've taken her under my wing, Mr King.

KING. So I noticed.

KEDGE. Yes, I've been teaching her all about mortality tables. I told her in case of fire or burglary, commission and damages come to her.

KING. I would hardly take Kedge's word as Gospel, Miss Todd.

KEDGE. You know I've got the best interests of the firm at heart, Mr King.

(KING *moves to Barrow and Horne*)

GIDNEY (*to Joyce*) Anyway, I'm thinking of moving on. You stay too long in a place you go daft. After all, with my qualifications I could go anywhere. (*He crosses to Albert*)

(JOYCE *rises and follows Gidney.*
    SEELEY *and* EILEEN *enter down* R *and stand at the downstage end of the bar*)

Couldn't I, Stokes?

ALBERT. What?

GIDNEY. I was saying, with my qualifications I could go anywhere. I could go anywhere and be anything.

ALBERT. So could I.

(*The samba music ceases*)

GIDNEY. Could you? What qualifications have you got?

ALBERT. Well, I've got a few, you know.

GIDNEY. Listen! Do you know that Chelsea wanted to sign me up a few years ago? They had a scout down to one of our games. They wanted to sign me up. And I'll tell you another thing, as well. I could turn professional cricketer any day I wanted to, if I wanted to.

ALBERT. Then why don't you?

GIDNEY. I don't want to.

JOYCE. You'd look lovely in white.

(*Quick step music is heard*)

GIDNEY. These people who talk about qualifications. Just make me laugh, that's all.

(GIDNEY *and* JOYCE *cross and join Seeley and Eileen at the bar.* KEDGE *and* BETTY *dance down* C. ALBERT *sits* C *of the sofa*)

KEDGE. Oh, you're lovely. You're the loveliest thing on four wheels.

(KING, BARROW *and* HORNE *cross to Ryan*)

KING (*to Horne and Barrow*) Well, I hope you'll both be in the team soon yourselves. I think it's a very good thing we've—that the firm's got a football team. And a cricket team, of course. It shows we look on the lighter side of things, too. Don't you agree?

HORNE. Oh, yes, Mr King.

BARROW. Yes, Mr King.

KING. Also gives a sense of belonging. Work together and play together. Office work can become too impersonal. We like to foster—to foster something—very different. You know what I mean?

HORNE. Oh, yes, Mr King.

BARROW. Yes, Mr King.

KING. You interested in sailing, by any chance? You're quite welcome to come down to my boat at Poole any week-end—do a bit of sailing along the coast.

BARROW. Oh, thank you, Mr King.

HORNE. Thank you, Mr King.

KING. Can I fill your glass, Ryan?

(RYAN *rises and moves with* KING *to the bar where* KING *pours a drink for Ryan.* BARROW *and* HORNE *move up* C)

Can't leave you without a drink, can we? The guest of honour.

(JOYCE *and* EILEEN *move down* RC. KEDGE *and* BETTY *dance up* LC)

JOYCE (*to Eileen; shyly*) Eh, what about going over and cheering up old Albert?

EILEEN. What for?

JOYCE. Well, he looks a bit gloomy, don't he?

EILEEN. I don't want to go over. You go over.

JOYCE. No, come on. You come over.
EILEEN. What for?
JOYCE. Cheer him up. For a bit of fun.
EILEEN. What for?
JOYCE. Come on. Come over.

(JOYCE *and* EILEEN *cross and sit either side of Albert on the sofa*)

Mind if we join you?
ALBERT. Oh, hullo.
EILEEN. Enjoying the party?
JOYCE. What are you sitting all gloomy about?
ALBERT. I'm not gloomy, I'm just sitting, drinking. Feel a bit tired, actually.
JOYCE. Why, what have you been doing?
ALBERT. Nothing.
JOYCE. You just said you were tired. Eh, move up, I'm on the edge.
ALBERT (*moving*) Sorry.
EILEEN. Eh, mind out, you're squashing me.
ALBERT. Oh . . .
JOYCE. You squash her, she won't mind.
EILEEN. Oh, Joyce!

(JOYCE *and* EILEEN *laugh.* GIDNEY *watches with a smile*)

JOYCE. Come on, tell me, what are you tired about?
ALBERT. Oh, just work, I suppose.
JOYCE. I've been working, too. I'm not tired. I love work. (*She leans across Albert to Eileen*) Don't you, Eileen?
EILEEN. Oh, yes, I love work.
ALBERT. No, I'm not tired, really. I'm all right.
EILEEN. He looks tired.
JOYCE. You've been living it up. Women.
EILEEN. I'll bet.
JOYCE. Females.

(EILEEN *and* JOYCE *giggle*)

ALBERT (*with an uncertain smile*) No, I wouldn't . . .
EILEEN. Eh, mind your drink. My best taffeta.
JOYCE. He's not bad looking when you get close.

EILEEN. Quite nice when you get close.
ALBERT. Thanks for the compliment.
EILEEN. You got a flat on your own?
ALBERT. No. Have you?
EILEEN (*forlornly*) No.
JOYCE. You live with your mother, don't you?

(KING *and* RYAN *cross to* LC *and* RYAN *sits in the armchair*)

ALBERT. Yes.
JOYCE. Does she look after you all right, then?
ALBERT. Yes, she . . . (*He rises*) I'm just going to the bar.
(*He crosses to the bar*)
JOYCE (*rising*) So are we.
EILEEN (*rising*) Me, too.

(JOYCE *and* EILEEN *follow Albert. The music ceases*)

KING (*crossing to* LC) Well now, everyone . . .
JOYCE. I'm having gin.

(BETTY *and* KEDGE *move to the sofa, sit and cuddle*)

ALBERT. Gin. Wait a minute . . .
KING. Just a minute, everyone—can I have you all here.

(JOYCE *moves and stands up* R *of Ryan.* EILEEN *moves and stands below Joyce.* GIDNEY *stands down* RC. BARROW *stands up* L *of Ryan.* HORNE *stands* L *of Ryan.* SEELEY *stands down* L *of Ryan*)

GIDNEY (*to Joyce*) Didn't make much impression, did you?
JOYCE. Didn't I?
KING. Just for a moment, please.
GIDNEY. Eh, Stokes, pay attention, will you?
ALBERT. What?
GIDNEY. Mr King wants your attention.
KING. Come along, Stokes.

(ALBERT *moves and stands below Eileen*)

I'd just like to propose a toast to our guest of honour—Mr Ryan. Gidney!
GIDNEY. Yes?

KING. Go and get Kedge out of that corner, will you?

(GIDNEY *crosses to the sofa*)

(*He moves down* C *and turns to face the others*) Now, as you know, we're all gathered here tonight to pay our respects to our old friend and colleague—Mr Ryan.

(KEDGE *and* BETTY *are locked together*)

GIDNEY (*tapping Kedge on the shoulder*) Mr Kedge, Mr King wants to know if you'll honour the party with your presence.

KEDGE (*jumping up*) Oh, sorry.

(BETTY, *thrown off, falls to the floor. The others laugh*)

Sorry. (*He helps Betty to her feet*)

(GIDNEY, KEDGE *and* BETTY *group* LC)

KING. We've all known Mr Ryan for a very long time. Of course, I've known him myself much longer than anyone here.

KEDGE (*singing*) For he's a jolly good fellow ...

KING. Wait! Very glad for your enthusiasm, Mr Kedge. Your heart, I am quite sure, is in the right place——

(*There is general laughter*)

—but please allow me to toast Mr Ryan first and then the floor is yours. Well, as I was saying, we are here tonight to pay tribute to a man who from time immemorial has become, how shall I put it, the very core of our little community. I remember Mr Ryan sitting at his very own desk the first time my father brought me into the office ...

(EILEEN *suddenly stiffens and gives a sharp scream. The others look at her*)

Good heavens!

GIDNEY. What is it?

OTHERS (*ad lib.*) What's happened? Eileen, what's the matter?

EILEEN. Someone touched me!

JOYCE. Touched you?

EILEEN. Someone touched me! Someone . . .
BETTY. What did he do?
KEDGE. Touched you? What did he do?
JOYCE. What did he do, Eileen?
EILEEN. He—he—he took a liberty!
KEDGE. Go on! Who did?

(EILEEN *turns and stares at Albert. There is a silence. The others stare at Albert*)

ALBERT. What are you looking at me for?
GIDNEY (*muttering*) Good God!

(*There is a tense, embarrassed pause*)

HORNE (*whispering to Barrow*) What did he do—touch her?
BARROW (*open-mouthed*) Yes.
HORNE (*wide-eyed*) Where?

(HORNE *and* BARROW *look at each other, open-mouthed and wide-eyed*)

ALBERT. What are you looking at me for?
KING (*moving up* RC) Please, now—can we possibly—I mean . . .

(EILEEN *takes a step towards Albert*)

EILEEN (*in a voice of reproach, indignation and horror*) Albert!
ALBERT. What do you mean?
SEELEY. How does she know it was Albert?
KEDGE. Wonder what he did. Made her jump, didn't he?
ALBERT (*backing down* C) Now look, wait a minute, this is absolutely ridiculous . . .
GIDNEY (*crossing to Albert*) Ridiculous, eh? I'll say it is. What do you think you're up to?
EILEEN. Yes, I was just standing there. Suddenly, this hand . . .
JOYCE. I could tell he was that sort.

(RYAN'S *hand rests comfortably on his knee. His face, smiling vaguely, is inclined to the ceiling. It is quite clear from his expression that it was his hand that strayed*)

GIDNEY (*pushing Albert* RC) Come in here, Albert.

ALBERT. Don't push me. What are you doing?

SEELEY. How do you know it was him?

ALBERT (*throwing off Gidney's hand*) Let go of me.

SEELEY (*crossing to Gidney*) What are you pushing him for?

GIDNEY. You keep out of this.

KING (*moving down* C; *nervously*) Now, please let me continue my toast, ladies and gentlemen. Really, you must settle this elsewhere.

SEELEY. We don't even know what he's supposed to have done.

ALBERT. I didn't do anything.

GIDNEY. We can guess what he did.

KING (*at speed*) We are all collected here tonight in honour of Mr Ryan and to present him with a token of our affection.

JOYCE (*to Albert*) You snake!

SEELEY. Well, what did he do? What's he supposed to have done?

ALBERT. She doesn't know what she's talking about.

SEELEY. Come on, what's he supposed to have done, Eileen, anyway?

EILEEN. Mind your own business.

JOYCE. You don't think she's going to tell you, do you?

GIDNEY. Look, Seeley, why don't you shut up?

SEELEY. Now, don't talk to me like that, Gidney.

ALBERT. Don't worry about him, Seeley.

KING. As I have been trying to say . . .

JOYCE. Sit down, Eileen. She's upset. Aren't you?

EILEEN (*to Seeley*) So would you be.

KING. Miss Phipps, would you mind composing yourself?

EILEEN. Composing myself!

KING. As I have been trying to say . . .

(ALBERT *crosses to the bar*)

KEDGE (*brightly*) I'm listening, Mr King.
KING. What?
KEDGE. I'm listening. I'm with you.
KING. Oh, thank you. Thank you, my boy.

(EILEEN, JOYCE, BARROW, HORNE, KEDGE, BETTY *and* KING *gather round Ryan. The* LIGHTS *fade a little on the group around Ryan*)

GIDNEY (*following Albert to the bar*) Wait a minute, Stokes.

(SEELEY *follows Gidney to the bar*)

ALBERT. What do you want?
GIDNEY (*crossing to* R *of Albert*) I haven't been satisfied with your—sort of—behaviour for some time. You know that, don't you?
ALBERT. You haven't . . . You haven't what?
GIDNEY. For instance, there was that bloody awful game of football you played when you threw the game away last Saturday, that I've got on my mind, besides one or two other things.
SEELEY. Eh, look, Gidney, you're talking like a prize . . .
GIDNEY (*viciously*) I've told you to keep out of this.
ALBERT (*moving down* R; *tensely*) I'm going, anyway.
GIDNEY (*intercepting Albert*) Wait a minute, let's have it out. What do you think you're up to?
ALBERT. Look, I've told you . . .
GIDNEY. What did you think you were doing with that girl?
ALBERT. I didn't touch her.
GIDNEY. I'm responsible for that girl. She's a good friend of mine. I know her uncle.
ALBERT. Do you?
SEELEY. You know, you're being so stupid, Gidney . . .
GIDNEY (*crossing to* R *of Seeley*) Seeley, I can take you any day, you know that, don't you?
SEELEY. Go on!
GIDNEY. Any day.
SEELEY. You can take me any day?
GIDNEY. Any day.

SEELEY. Well, go on, then. Go on—if you can take me . . .

ALBERT. Seeley . . .

SEELEY. No. If he says he can take me, if he can take me any day . . .

ALBERT. Gidney, why don't you—why don't you get back to the party?

GIDNEY. I was telling you, Albert . . .

ALBERT. "Stokes."

GIDNEY. I was telling you, Albert, that if you're going to behave like a boy of ten in mixed company . . .

ALBERT. I told you my name's "Stokes"!

GIDNEY. Don't be childish, Albert!

ALBERT (*moving down* R) Good night.

GIDNEY (*intercepting Albert*) Go back and apologize.

ALBERT. What for?

GIDNEY. For insulting a lady—mate. A lady. Something to do with breeding. But I suppose you're too bloody backward to know anything about that.

ALBERT. You're talking right out of your hat.

SEELEY. Right out of the bowler.

GIDNEY (*to Seeley*) No-one invited you in here, did they?

SEELEY. Who invited you?

GIDNEY. I'm talking to this man on behalf of the firm. Unless I get a satisfactory explanation I shall think seriously about recommending his dismissal.

ALBERT. Get out of my way, will you?

GIDNEY. Acting like an animal all over the place.

ALBERT. Move out of it!

GIDNEY (*breathlessly*) I know your trouble.

ALBERT. Oh, yes?

GIDNEY. Yes, sticks out a mile.

ALBERT. Does it?

GIDNEY. Yes.

ALBERT. What's my trouble, then?

GIDNEY (*very deliberately*) You're a mother's boy. That's what you are. That's your trouble. You're a mother's boy.

(ALBERT *hits Gidney. There is a scuffle.* SEELEY *tries to part them. The three rock back and forth. There are confused blows, words and grunts.* KING *crosses to* RC)

KING. What in heaven's name is going on here?

The scuffle stops. There is a short silence. ALBERT *turns and exits down* R *as—*

the LIGHTS BLACK-OUT

SCENE VI

SCENE—*The kitchen.*

When the LIGHTS *come up, it is midnight.* MRS STOKES *is seated above the table, asleep, her head resting on the table. A disordered pack of playing cards is on the table.* ALBERT *enters down the stairs, sees Mrs Stokes, turns and creeps off with great stealth.* MRS STOKES *wakes.*

MRS STOKES (*calling*) Albert!

(ALBERT *stops*)

Albert! Is that you? (*She rises and goes to the stairs*) What are you creeping up the stairs for? Might have been a burglar. What would I have done, then? Creeping up the stairs like that. Give anyone a fright. Creeping up the stairs like that. You leave me in the house all alone . . .

(ALBERT *enters down the stairs*)

(*She looks at him*) Look at you! Look at your suit—what's the matter with your tie, it's all crumpled—I pressed it for you this morning.

(ALBERT *crosses to the sink, pours himself a glass of water and drinks*)

Well, I won't even ask any questions. That's all. You look a disgrace. What have you been doing—mucking about with girls? (*She moves to the table and packs up the cards*) Mucking about with girls, I suppose. Do you know what the time is? I fell asleep, right here at this table, waiting

for you. I don't know what your father would say. Coming
in this time of night. It's after twelve o'clock. In a state
like that.

(ALBERT *moves and sits* L *of the table*)

Drunk, I suppose. I suppose your dinner's ruined. Well,
if you want to make a convenience out of your own home,
that's your business. I'm only your mother. I don't suppose
that counts for much these days. I'm not saying any more.
If you want to go mucking about with girls, that's your
business. (*She goes to the stove and takes Albert's dinner from the
oven*) Well, anyway, you'll have your dinner. You haven't
eaten a single thing all night. (*She puts the food on the table in
front of Albert*) I wouldn't mind if you found a really nice
girl and brought her home and introduced her to your
mother, brought her home for dinner, I'd know you were
sincere, if she was a really nice girl, she'd be like a daughter
to me. But you've never brought a girl home here in your
life. I suppose you're ashamed of your mother. (*She pauses
and moves up* R *of the table*) Come on, it's all dried up. I
kept it on a low light. I couldn't even go up to grandma's
room and have a look round because there wasn't any bulb.
You might as well eat it.

(ALBERT *pushes his plate aside*)

What's the matter, are you drunk? Where did you go, to
one of those pubs in the West End? You'll get into serious
trouble, my boy, if you frequent those places, I'm warning
you. Don't you read the papers? (*She pauses*) I hope you're
satisfied, anyway. The house in darkness, I wasn't going
to break my neck going down to that cellar to look for a
bulb, you come home looking like I don't know what, anyone would think you gave me a fortune out of your wages.
Yes. I don't say anything, do I? I keep quiet about what
you expect me to manage on. I never grumble. I keep a
lovely home, I bet there's none of the boys in your firm
better fed than you are. I'm not asking for gratitude. But
one thing hurts me, Albert, and I'll tell you what it is. Not
for years, not for years, have you come up to me and said,
"Mum, I love you," like you did when you were a little boy.

You've never said it without me having to ask you. Not since before your father died. And he was a good man. He had high hopes of you. I've never told you, Albert, about the high hopes he had of you. I don't know what you do with all your money. But don't forget what it cost us to rear you, my boy, I've never told you about the sacrifices we made, you wouldn't care, anyway. Telling me lies about going to the firm's party. They've got a bit of respect at that firm, that's why we sent you there, to start off your career, they wouldn't let you carry on like that at one of their functions. Mr King would have his eye on you. I don't know where you've been. Well, if you don't want to lead a clean life it's your look-out, if you want to go mucking about with all sorts of bits of girls, if you're content to leave your own mother sitting here till midnight, and I wasn't feeling well, anyway, I didn't tell you because I didn't want to upset you, I keep things from you, you're the only one I've got, but what do you care, you don't care, you don't care, the least you can do is to eat the dinner I cooked for you, especially for you, it's shepherd's pie.

ALBERT *suddenly rises, grabs the clock and raises it violently above his head.* MRS STOKES *gives a stifled scream as—*

the LIGHTS *fade on the kitchen and come up on the coffee-stall*

SCENE VII

SCENE—*The coffee-stall.*

When the LIGHTS *come up, the coffee-stall is shuttered. A clock strikes the three-quarters.* ALBERT *enters down* L *and crosses to the coffee-stall. The* GIRL *enters above the coffee-stall and smiles seductively at Albert.*

GIRL. Good evening. (*She pauses*) What are you doing? (*She pauses*) What are you doing out at this time of night? (*She moves closer to Albert*) I live just round the corner.

(ALBERT *stares at her*)

Like to? Chilly out here, isn't it? Come on. (*She pauses*)
Come on.

ALBERT *and the* GIRL *exit up* R *as—*

the LIGHTS *fade on the coffee-stall and come up on the
bedroom*

SCENE VIII

SCENE—*The Girl's bedroom.*

When the LIGHTS *come up, the whistle and sounds of a passing
train are heard. The* GIRL *enters. Her manner has changed
from the seductive. She is brisk and nervous.*

GIRL. Come in. Don't slam the door. Shut it gently.

(ALBERT *enters and crosses to* R)

I'll light the fire. (*She goes to the fire*) Chilly, out, don't you
find? Have you got a match?

(ALBERT *crosses to the Girl*)

Please don't walk so heavily. Please. There's no need to
let—to let the whole house know you're here. Life's difficult
enough as it is. (*She looks on the mantelpiece*) Have you got
a match?
   ALBERT (*moving down* C) No, I—I don't think I have.
   GIRL. Oh, God, you'd think you'd have a match.

(ALBERT *crosses to the chair* R)

I say, would you mind taking your shoes off? You're
really making a dreaful row. Really, I can't bear—noisy—
people.

(ALBERT *looks at his shoes and begins to untie one*)

(*She searches for the matches*) I know I had one somewhere.
   ALBERT. I've got a lighter. (*He removes one shoe*)
   GIRL (*turning*) You can't light a gas-fire with a lighter.

You'd burn your fingers. (*She turns to the mantelpiece*) Where are the damn things? This is ridiculous. (*She bends down to the hearth*) I die without the fire. I simply die. (*She finds the matches in the hearth*) Ah, here we are. (*She strikes a match*) At last. (*She turns on the gas-fire and lights it, then puts the matches on the mantelpiece, picks up a photograph and turns to Albert*) Do you like this photo? (*She crosses to Albert*) It's my little girl. She's staying with friends. Rather fine, isn't she? Very aristocratic features, don't you think? She's at a very select boarding-school at the moment, actually. In— Hereford, very near Hereford. (*She crosses and replaces the photograph on the mantelpiece*) I shall be going down for the Prize Day shortly. (*She turns to Albert*) You do look idiotic standing there with one shoe on and one shoe off. All lop-sided.

(ALBERT *bends down, pulls at the lace of the other shoe. The lace breaks. He swears shortly under his breath*)

(*Sharply*) Do you mind not saying words like that?
ALBERT. I didn't . . .
GIRL. I heard you curse.
ALBERT. My lace broke. (*He takes off the other shoe and puts both shoes under the chair* R)
GIRL. That's no excuse.
ALBERT. What did I say?
GIRL. I'm sorry, I can't bear that sort of thing. It's just —not in my personality.
ALBERT. I'm sorry.
GIRL. It's quite all right. (*She crosses to Albert*) It's just —something in my nature. I've got to think of my daughter, too, you know. Come near the fire a minute. Sit down.

(ALBERT *crosses to the fire and goes to sit on the stool* L)

Not on that! That's my seat. It's my own stool. I did the needlework myself. A long time ago.

(ALBERT *sits on the left end of the bed*)

(*She crosses to the fire*) Which do you prefer, electric or gas? For a fire, I mean?
ALBERT (*holding his forehead; muttering*) I don't know.

GIRL. There's no need to be rude—it was a civil question. I prefer gas. Or a log fire, of course. They have them in Switzerland.

(*There is a pause*)

Have you got a headache?

ALBERT. No.

GIRL. I didn't realize you had a lighter. You don't happen to have any cigarettes on you, I suppose?

ALBERT (*turning away*) No.

GIRL. I'm very fond of a smoke. After dinner. With a glass of wine. Or before dinner, with sherry. (*She moves to Albert*) You look as if you've had a night out. Where have you been? Had a nice time?

ALBERT (*rising and crossing to the chair* R) Quite—quite nice.

GIRL. What do you do?

ALBERT (*sitting on the chair* R) I—work in films.

GIRL (*sitting on the stool*) Films? Really? What do you do?

ALBERT. I'm an assistant director.

GIRL. Really? How funny. I used to be a continuity girl. But I gave it up.

ALBERT (*tonelessly*) What a pity.

GIRL. Yes, I'm beginning to think you're right. You meet such a good class of people. Of course, now you say you're an assistant director, I can see what you mean. I mean, I could tell you had breeding the moment I saw you. You looked a bit washed out, perhaps, but there was no mistaking the fact that you had breeding. I'm extremely particular, you see. I do like a certain amount of delicacy in men—a certain amount—a certain degree—a certain amount of refinement. You do see my point? Some men I couldn't possibly entertain. Not even if I was—starving. I don't want to be personal, but that word you used, when you broke your lace, it made me shiver, I'm just not that type, made me wonder if you were as well-bred as I thought.

(ALBERT *wipes his face with his hand*)

(*She rises and crosses to Albert*) You do look hot. Why are you so hot? It's chilly. Yes. You remind me. (*She looks out of the window*) I saw the most ghastly, horrible fight before—there was a man, one man, he was sweating—sweating. (*She turns to Albert*) You haven't been in a fight, by any chance? I don't know how men can be so bestial. It's hardly much fun for women, I can tell you. I don't want someone else's blood on my carpet. (*She sits on the bed*)

(ALBERT *chuckles*)

What are you laughing at?
ALBERT. Nothing.
GIRL. It's not in the least funny.

(ALBERT *looks at the mantelpiece*)

What are you looking at?
ALBERT (*rising and crossing to the mantelpiece; ruminatively*) That's a nice big clock.

(*The clock shows twenty past two*)

GIRL (*with fatigue*) Yes, it's late. I suppose we might as well . . . Haven't you got a cigarette?
ALBERT. No.
GIRL (*jumping up*) I'm sure I have, somewhere. (*She looks under the pillow and takes out a packet of cigarettes and a box of matches*) Yes, here we are, I knew I had. I have to hide them. The woman who comes in to do my room, she's very light-fingered. I don't know why she comes in at all. Nobody wants her, all she does is spy on me, but I'm obliged to put up with her, this room is serviced. (*She moves down* C) Which means I have to pay a pretty penny. (*She lights a cigarette*) It's a dreadful area, too. I'm thinking of moving. The neighbourhood is full of people of no class at all. I just don't fit it.
ALBERT. Is that clock right?
GIRL. People have told me, the most distinguished people, that I could go anywhere. (*She moves to Albert*) "You could go anywhere," they've told me, "you could be anything." I'm quite well educated, you know. My father was a—he was a military man. In the army. (*She*

sits on the left end of the bed) Actually, it was a relief to speak to you. I haven't—spoken to anyone for some hours.

(ALBERT *suddenly coughs violently*)

Oh, please don't do that! Use your handkerchief.

(ALBERT *sighs and groans and crosses to the chair* R)

What on earth's the matter with you? What have you been doing tonight?

(ALBERT *looks at the Girl and smiles*)

ALBERT (*sitting on the chair* R) Nothing.
GIRL. Really? (*She belches*) Oh, excuse me. I haven't eaten all day. I had a tooth out. Hiccups come from not eating, don't they? Do you—do you want one of these? (*She tosses a cigarette to Albert*)

(ALBERT *slowly lights a cigarette*)

(*She rises, removes her skirt and blouse and puts on a wrap*) I mean, I'm no different from any other girls. In fact, I'm better. These so-called respectable girls, for instance, I'm sure they're much worse than I am. Well, you're an assistant director—all your continuity girls and secretaries, I'll bet they're—very loose.
ALBERT. Uh.
GIRL. Do you know what I've actually heard? I've heard that respectable married women, solicitors' wives, go out and pick men up when their husbands are out on business. Isn't that fantastic? I mean, they're supposed to be— they're supposed to be respectable.
ALBERT (*muttering*) Fantastic.
GIRL. I beg your pardon?
ALBERT. I said it was fantastic.
GIRL. It is. You're right. Quite fantastic. Here's one thing, though. There's one thing that's always fascinated me. How far do men's girl friends go? I've often won-dered. (*She pauses*) Eh?
ALBERT. Depends.
GIRL. Yes, I suppose it must. (*She pauses*) You mean on the girl?

ALBERT. What?

GIRL. You mean it depends on the girl?

ALBERT. It would do—yes.

GIRL. Quite possibly. I must admit that with your continuity girls and secretaries, I don't see why you—had to approach me. Have you been on the town tonight, then? With a continuity girl?

ALBERT (*rising*) You're a bit—worried about continuity girls, aren't you?

GIRL. Only because I've been one myself. I know what they're like. No better than they should be.

ALBERT. When were you a . . . ?

GIRL (*moving to the head of the bed*) Years ago. (*She sits on the bed*) You're nosey, aren't you? (*She looks out of the window*) Sometimes I wish the night would never end. I like sleeping. I could sleep—on and on.

(*The sound of a passing train is heard.* ALBERT *crosses to the mantelpiece and picks up the clock*)

Yes, you can see the station from here. All the trains go out, right through the night.

(ALBERT *stares at the clock*)

(*She rises and removes the counterpane*) I suppose we might as well . . . (*She turns and looks at Albert*) What are you doing? (*She moves to him*) What are you doing with that clock?

(ALBERT *slowly looks at her*)

Mmmm?

ALBERT. Admiring it.

GIRL. It's a perfectly ordinary clock. Give me it. I've seen too many people slip things into their pockets before now, as soon as your back's turned.

(ALBERT *hands the clock to her and crosses to* RC)

(*She puts the clock on the mantelpieace*) Mind your ash—don't spill it all over the floor. I have to keep this carpet immaculate. Otherwise the charlady . . . She's always looking for excuses for telling tales. (*She takes an ashtray from the*

mantelpiece and gives it to Albert) Here. Here's an ashtray.
Use it, please.

(ALBERT *stares at her*)

Sit down. Sit down. Don't stand about like that. What
are you staring at me for?

(ALBERT *sits on the bed*)

(*She studies him*) Where's your wife?
ALBERT. Nowhere.

(*The* GIRL *takes the ashtray, stubs out her cigarette and puts
the ashtray on the mantelpiece*)

GIRL. And what films are you making at the moment?
ALBERT. I'm on holiday.
GIRL. Where do you work?
ALBERT. I'm a freelance.
GIRL. You're—rather young to be in such a—high
position, aren't you?
ALBERT. Oh?
GIRL (*laughing*) You amuse me. You interest me. I'm a
bit of a psychologist, you know. You're very young to be—
what you said you were. (*She moves to Albert and lifts his chin*)
There's something childish in your face, almost retarded.
(*She laughs*) I do like that word. I'm not being personal,
of course—just being—psychological. Of course, I can see
you're one for the girls. Don't know why you had to pick
on me, at this time of night—really rather forward of you.
I'm a respectable mother, you know—(*she glances at the
photograph*) with a child at boarding-school. You couldn't
call me—anything else. All I do, I just entertain a few
gentlemen, of my own choice, now and again. What girl
doesn't?

(ALBERT *screws up his cigarette and lets it fall to the floor*)

(*Outraged*) What do you think you're doing? (*She stares at
him*) Pick it up! Pick that up, I tell you! It's my carpet.
(*She lunges towards the cigarette*) It's not my carpet, they'll
make me pay.

(ALBERT *grabs the Girl's wrist*)

What are you doing? Let go! Treating my place like a
pigsty.

(ALBERT *grabs her other wrist*)

(*She looks up at Albert as he bends over her*) Let me go! You're
burning my carpet! (*She stamps on the cigarette*)
ALBERT (*quietly and intensely*) Sit down. (*He forces her on
to the stool*)
GIRL. How dare you!
ALBERT. Shut up. Sit down!
GIRL (*struggling*) What are you doing?
ALBERT (*erratically, trembling, but with quiet command*) Don't
scream. I'm warning you. No screaming. I warn you.
GIRL. What's the . . . ?
ALBERT (*through his teeth*) Be quiet. I told you to be
quiet. Now you be quiet.
GIRL. What are you going to do?
ALBERT (*seizing the clock from the mantelpiece*) Don't muck
me about!

(*The* GIRL *freezes with terror*)

See this? One crack with this—just one crack . . . (*Viciously*)
Who do you think you are? You talk too much, you know
that. You never stop talking. Just because you're a woman,
you think you can get away with it. (*He bends over her*)
You've made a mistake this time. You've picked the wrong
man. (*He begins to grow in stature and excitement, passing the
clock from hand to hand*) You're all the same, you see,
you're all the same, you're just a dead weight round my
neck. What makes you think . . . ? (*He moves about the room,
at one point half crouching, at another standing upright, as if
exercising his body*) What makes you think you can—tell
me . . . ? Yes. It's the same as this business about the
light in grandma's room. Always something. Always
something. (*He moves to her*) My ash? I'll put it where I
like. You see this clock? Watch your step. Just watch your
step.
GIRL. Stop this. (*She starts to rise*)

(ALBERT *pushes her back on to the stool*)

What are you . . . ?

(ALBERT *seizes her wrist, with trembling, controlled violence*)

ALBERT. Watch your step! (*Stammering*) I've had—I've had—I've had—just about enough. Get it? "What would your father say, Albert?" "What would . . . ?" So you know what I did? (*He looks at her and chuckles*) Don't be so frightened.

GIRL. I . . .

ALBERT (*casually*) Don't be frightened. (*He squats by her, still holding the clock*) I'm just telling you. I'm just telling you, that's all. (*Breathlessly*) You haven't got any breeding. She hadn't, either. And what about those girls tonight? Same kind. And that one. I didn't touch her.

GIRL (*almost inaudibly*) What have you been doing?

ALBERT. I've got as many qualifications as the next man. Let's get that quite—straight. And I got the answer to her. I got the answer to her, you see, tonight—I finished the conversation—I finished it—I finished her. (*He rises slowly*)

(*The* GIRL *squirms*)

(*He raises the clock*) With this clock! (*He trembles*) One —crack—with—this—clock—finished. (*Thoughtfully*) Of course, I loved her, really. (*He suddenly puts the clock on the mantelpiece, sees the photograph, picks it up and looks curiously at it*)

(*The* GIRL *rises and crosses to* R)

Uhhh! Your daughter? This is a photo of your daughter? Uhhh? (*He breaks the frame and extracts the photograph*)

GIRL (*rushing at him*) Leave that!

(ALBERT *drops the frame and looks at the photograph*)

ALBERT. Is it?

(*The* GIRL *grabs at the photograph.* ALBERT *grabs her wrist and holds her at arm's length*)

GIRL. Leave that! (*She writhes*) Don't—it's mine.

(ALBERT *releases her, turns the photograph over and reads from the back*)

ALBERT. "Class Three Classical. Third prize, Bronze Medal, Twickenham Competition, nineteen thirty-three." (*He stares at the Girl*)

(*The* GIRL *stands shivering and whimpering*)

You liar! That's you.

GIRL. It's not.

ALBERT. That's not your daughter. It's you. You're just a fake, you're just all lies.

GIRL (*rushing at him*) Scum! Filthy scum!

(ALBERT *pushes her on to the bed*)

ALBERT (*warningly*) Mind how you talk to me. (*He crumples the photograph*)

GIRL (*moaning*) My daughter. My little girl. My little baby girl.

ALBERT. Get up!

GIRL. No . . .

ALBERT. Get up! Up!

(*The* GIRL *rises*)

(*He points* L) Walk over there. Go on. Get over there. Do as you're told. Do as I'm telling you. I'm giving the orders here.

(*The* GIRL *backs to the mantelpiece*)

Stop!

GIRL (*whimpering*) What—you want me to do?

ALBERT (*moving to the foot of the bed*) Just keep your big mouth shut, for a start. (*He frowns uncertainly*) Cover your face.

(*The* GIRL *puts her hands in front of her face*)

(*He looks about, blinking, unsure of what to do*) Yes. That's right. (*He sees his shoes*) Those shoes. Pick them up. Come on, come on. Those shoes—pick them up.

(*The* GIRL *crosses to* R *and picks up Albert's shoes*)

That's right. Bring them over here. Come on. (*He sits on the stool and stretches out his legs*) That's right. Put them on.

(*The* LIGHTS *come up slowly for dawn effect*)

GIRL (*crossing to Albert*) You're . . .

(*The gas-fire suddenly goes out*)

ALBERT. On! Right on!

(*The* GIRL *kneels and puts Albert's shoes on for him*)

That's it. That's it. That's more like it. That's—more like it! Doesn't matter if the lace is broken, there's enough to tie. Quite enough. Good. Good. (*He rises*)

(*The* GIRL *crouches on the floor. There is a silence*)

(*He shivers, murmurs with the cold and looks about the room*) It's cold. (*He pauses*) Ooh, it's freezing.

GIRL (*whimpering*) The fire's gone.

ALBERT (*looking out of the window at the dawn*) What's that? Looks like light. Ooh, it's perishing. (*He looks around. Muttering*) What a dump. (*He goes to the mantelpiece, picks up the clock, looks at it then throws it down*) Not staying here. Getting out of this place. (*He smiles. Softly*) So you—bear that in mind. Mind how you talk to me. (*He moves up* C, *turns, takes half a crown from his pocket and flips it to the Girl*) Buy yourself a seat—buy yourself a seat at a circus.

ALBERT *exits as—*

the LIGHTS *fade on the bedroom and come up on the kitchen*

SCENE IX

SCENE—*The kitchen.*

When the LIGHTS *come up, the kitchen is empty.* ALBERT *enters. He has a slight smile on his face. He removes his jacket and tie, throws them across the room, then sits heavily and loosely on the chair* L *of the table and stretches out his legs. He stretches out his arms, yawns luxuriously, scratches his head with both hands then stares ruminatively at the ceiling, with a smile on his face.*

MRS STOKES (*off; calling*) Albert! (*She pauses*) Albert!

(ALBERT'S *body freezes. His gaze comes down. His legs slowly come together and he looks in front of him.*

   MRS STOKES *enters, moves to* R *of the table and stands looking at Albert. She is in her dressing-gown*)

Do you know what the time is? (*She pauses*) Where have you been? (*She pauses. Reproachfully and near to tears*) I don't know what to say to you, Albert. To raise your hand to your own mother. You've never done that before in your life. To threaten your own mother. (*She pauses and takes a step towards Albert*) That clock would have hurt me, Albert. And you'd have been—I know you'd have been very sorry. Aren't I a good mother to you? Everything I do is—is for your own good. You should know that. You're all I've got. (*She looks at his slumped figure and her reproach turns to solicitude. Gently*) Look at you. You look washed out. Oh, you look . . . I don't understand what could have come over you. (*She moves the chair above the table close to Albert, sits and takes his arm*) Listen, Albert, I'll tell you what I'm going to do. I'm going to forget it. You see? I'm going to forget all about it. We'll have your holiday in a fortnight. We can go away. (*She strokes his hand*) We'll go away— together. (*She pauses*)

   (*The* LIGHTS *dim a little*)

It's not as if you're a bad boy—you're a good boy—I know you are—it's not as if you're really bad, Albert, you're not you're not bad, you're good—you're not a bad boy, Albert, I know you're not. (*She rises and puts her arms around Albert's shoulders*) You're good, you're not bad, you're a good boy—I know you are. (*She pauses*) You are, aren't you?

CURTAIN

FURNITURE AND PROPERTY LIST

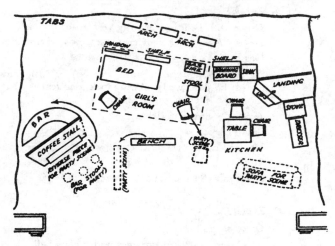

SCENE I

On stage: *In kitchen:*

Sink

Draining-board. *On it:* 3 tumblers, plastic plate-rack with clean crockery

Under draining-board: shoe polish, shoe brushes, shoe polisher

Shelf (over draining-board) *On it:* large old-fashioned alarm clock, mirror, hairbrush

Gas stove. *On it:* oven cloth, frying-pan, kettle, saucepan

In oven: baking dish, Albert's dinner (Shepherd's Pie)

Kitchen cabinet. *On shelf:* pile of clean linen including tie, clean handkerchief, clothes brush. *In drawer:* cutlery, pack of cards

Table. *On it :* 2 side plates, 2 each knives, forks and spoons

In bedroom :

Divan with bedding, ashtray with stubs and ash
Under pillow : packet of cigarettes, box of matches
Gas fire
On mantelpiece : photograph (framed) of little girl (to be destroyed), alarm clock identical to that in the kitchen, other dressing
In hearth : box of matches
Small carpet
Upright chair. *On it :* dressing-gown
Stool with embroidered top
Armchair (for use in party scene)

Coffee-stall :

On counter :

Cheese rolls and sausages under glass bell
4 cups
2 plates
Brown teapot with tea
White jug with milk
Sugar bowl with sugar and spoon
Coins in saucer
On shelf : cigarettes, chocolate, etc., for dressing, newspaper, teacloth
Wooden bench (c)
On bar (back of truck): bottles of whisky, gin, beer and minerals, syphon of soda, 11 glasses

Off stage : 3 high stools (for party scene)
Sofa (for party scene)

Personal: ALBERT: half a crown, cigarette lighter, comb, handkerchief

SCENE II

Personal: SEELEY: half a crown

SCENE III

Setting as Scene I

SCENE IV

Setting as Scene II
Personal: KEDGE: packet of cigarettes, lighter
SEELEY: coins

SCENE V

During BLACK-OUT:
Revolve truck to reveal bar
Set: Bench from C to RC
Armchair from rostrum to LC
Sofa (L)
3 tall stools at bar

SCENE VI

During BLACK-OUT:
Revolve truck to reveal coffee-stall
Strike: Armchair
Sofa

Bar stools
Bench

Set: *On kitchen table:* playing cards

SCENE VII

Coffee-stall shuttered

SCENE VIII

Bedroom setting c

SCENE IX

Setting as Scene VI

LIGHTING PLOT

Property fittings required: gas fire

SCENE I. Interior. A kitchen. Evening

To open: The stage in darkness

Cue 1 At rise of Curtain (**Page** 1)
Bring up lights on kitchen area L

Cue 2 MRS STOKES: ". . . game of rummy?" (**Page** 6)
Fade lights on kitchen L
Bring up lights on coffee-stall R

SCENE II. Exterior. A coffee-stall. Evening

To open: Effect of twilight

Cue 3 OLD MAN: ". . . compressed, I thought." (**Page** 10)
Fade lights on coffee-stall
Bring up lights on kitchen

SCENE III. Interior. The kitchen. Evening

To open: Lights as Scene I

Cue 4 MRS STOKES: ". . . like a gentleman." (**Page** 11)
Fade lights on kitchen
Bring up lights on coffee-stall

SCENE IV. Exterior. The coffee-stall. Evening

To open: Lights as Scene II

Cue 5 SEELEY, KEDGE and ALBERT exit (**Page** 16)
BLACK-OUT

SCENE V. Interior. A lounge. Night

Cue 6 When Scene set (**Page** 16)
Bring up lights

Cue 7   KING: "Thank you, my boy."   (Page 27)
            Fade lights a little on group C

Cue 8   ALBERT exits   (Page 29)
            BLACK-OUT

SCENE VI.   Interior. The kitchen. Night

Cue 9   When Scene set   (Page 29)
            Bring up lights on kitchen

Cue 10   MRS STOKES screams   (Page 31)
            Fade lights on kitchen
            Bring up lights to ½ on coffee-stall

SCENE VII. Exterior. The coffee-stall. Night

To open : Lights at ½

Cue 11   ALBERT and the GIRL exit   (Page 32)
            Fade lights on coffee-stall
            Bring up lights on bedroom

SCENE VIII. Interior. A bedroom. Night

To open : Effect of artificial light

Cue 12   The GIRL lights the gas fire   (Page 33)
            Bring in fire glow

Cue 13   ALBERT: "Put them on."   (Page 42)
            Bring up lights slowly for dawn effect

Cue 14   GIRL: "You're . . ."   (Page 42)
            Dim out fire glow

Cue 15   ALBERT exits   (Page 42)
            Fade lights on bedroom
            Bring up lights on kitchen

SCENE IX. Interior. The kitchen

To open : Effect of dawn

Cue 16   MRS STOKES: ". . . go away—together." .   (Page 43)
            Fade lights to ½

EFFECTS PLOT

SCENE I

Cue 1   At rise of CURTAIN   (Page 1)
Sound of train and train whistle

SCENE II

No cues

SCENE III

No cues

SCENE IV

No cues

SCENE V

Cue 2   At opening of Scene   (Page 16)
Dance music. A Quick Step

Cue 3   KING: ". . . make yourself comfortable."   (Page 17)
Dance music ceases

Cue 4   GIDNEY: "Do you think so?"   (Page 18)
Samba music

Cue 5   ALBERT: "So could I."   (Page 20)
Samba music ceases

Cue 6   JOYCE: ". . . lovely in white."   (Page 20)
Quick Step music

| *Cue* 7 | EILEEN: "Me, too." | (Page 23) |
| | *Music ceases* | |

SCENE VI

| *Cue* 8 | As lights come up on kitchen | (Page 29) |
| | *Clock strikes* 12 | |

SCENE VII

No cues

SCENE VIII

Cue 9	As lights come up on bedroom	(Page 32)
	Sound of train and train whistle	
Cue 10	GIRL: ". . . on and on."	(Page 37)
	Sound of train passing	

SCENE IX

No cues

MADE AND PRINTED IN GREAT BRITAIN BY
LATIMER TREND & COMPANY LTD PLYMOUTH

MADE IN ENGLAND